Under the Ground

Words by Eugene Booth

Pictures by Derek Collard

RAINTREE CHILDRENS BOOKS
Milwaukee • Toronto • Melbourne • London

Library of Congress Number: 77-8037

1 2 3 4 5 6 7 8 9 0 81 80 79 78 77

Printed and bound in the United States of America.

Library of Congress Cataloging in Publication Data

Booth, Eugene, 1940 —
 Under the ground.

 (A Raintree spotlight book)
 SUMMARY: Pictures and questions stimulate discussion about animals, tunnels, pipes, and even men underground.
 [1. Underground utility lines. 2. Underground construction. 3. Animals. 4. Caves] I. Collard, Derek. II. Title.
PZ7.B6467Ul [E]   77-8037
ISBN 0-8393-0110-3 lib. bdg.

Under the Ground

Which animals are under the ground?
Which ones are above the ground?

Which animals are chasing the others?
What do you think could happen next?
Turn the page and see.

Which animals got caught?
Which ones got away?
What else do you see in the picture?

How many animals have four legs?
Which ones do not have legs at all?
How many have wings?

Count the animals that live in holes.
1 badger, 2 foxes, 3 snakes, 4 moles.

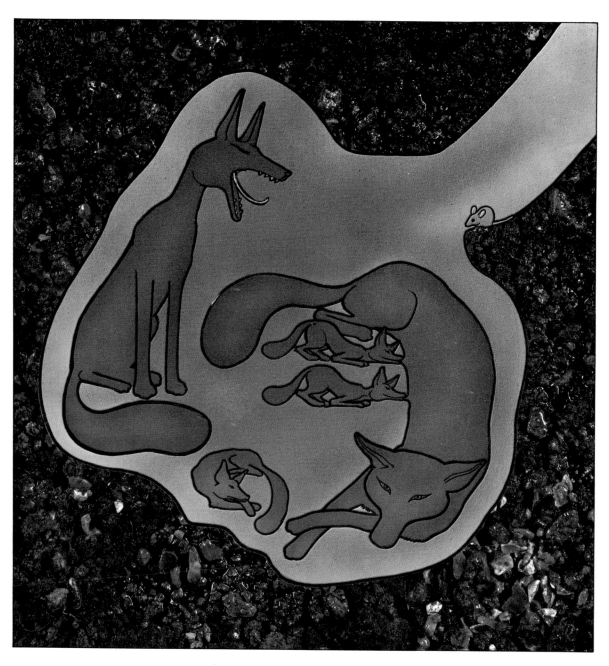

How many foxes are in this family?
What is each fox doing?
Can you find another animal?

How many mice are in each hole?
Which hole has more than three?
How many mice are there in all?

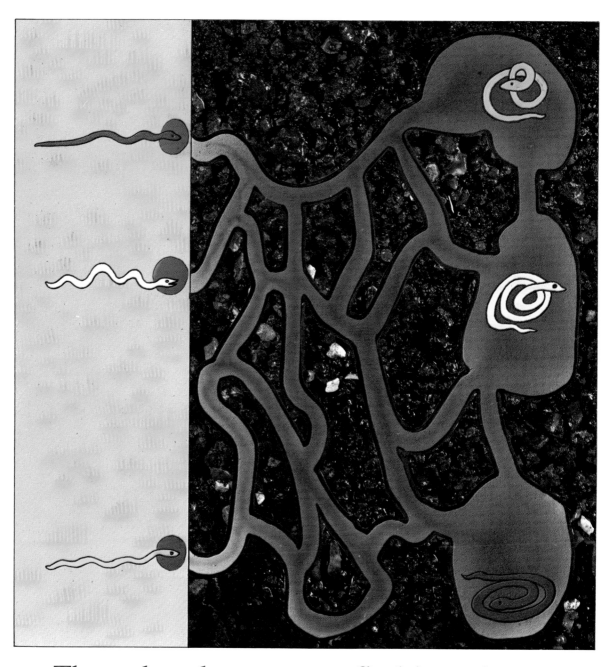

The red snake wants to find its twin.
So do the green and yellow snakes.
Can you show each snake the way?

Which train is above the ground?
Which train is farthest down?
Which train has the most cars?

There is a tunnel in each picture.
Why is it being made?
Where will each tunnel end?

What things are lying in the dirt?
Do you see animals and plants?
What things were made by people?

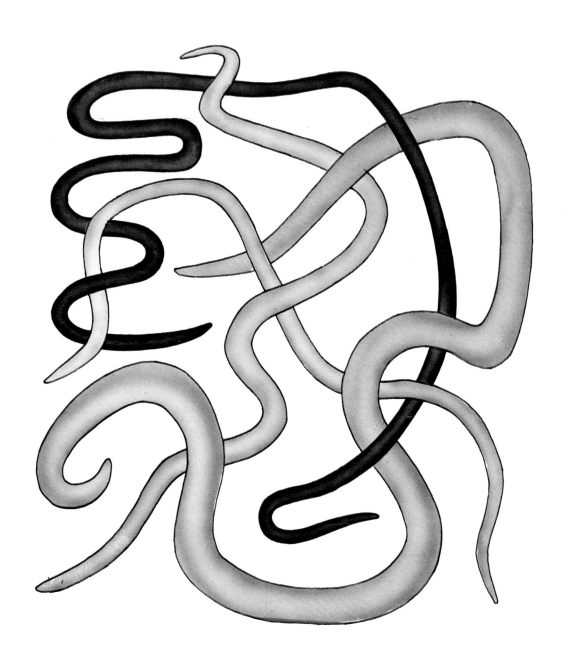

How many worms can you see?
Can you trace each worm
from one end to the other?
Which worm do you think is longest?

This picture shows the pipes in a house.
Where does the clean water come from?
Where does the dirty water go?

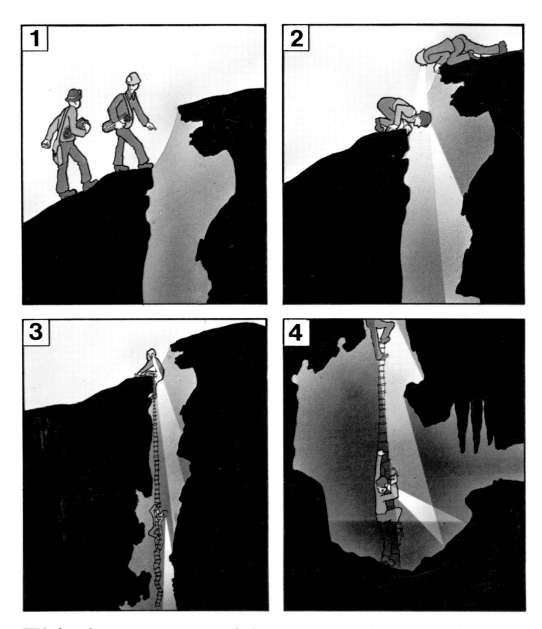

This is a story without words. Look at each picture. Tell what is going on. What will happen next?

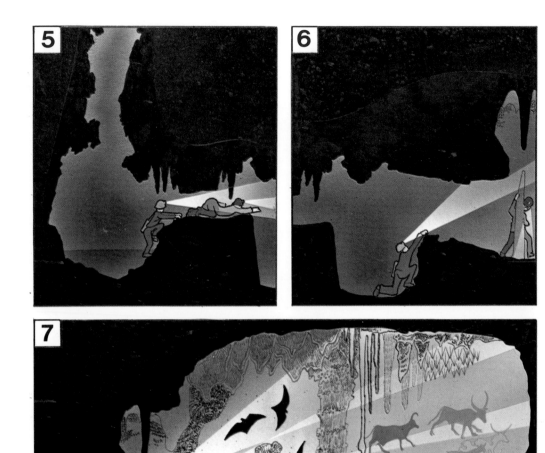

How do the men see?
What do they find in the cave?
Has someone been in this cave before?

Here are some bright stones
from the cave. Look at the shapes below.
Can you find these shapes in the stones?

19

How many holes did the man dig?
What did he put in each hole?
Tell the story from the pictures.

What foods grow under the ground?
What foods grow above?
Which of these foods do you like to eat?